2024 HONOLULU TRAVEL GUIDE

ULTIMATE GUIDE TO OAHU REVEALING HONOLULU, WAIKIKI & BEYOND

Richard Stephen

Copyright © 2023 by Richard Stephen. All rights reserved. This book or any portion thereof may not be reproduced or used in any manner whatsoever without the express written permission of the publisher except for the use of brief quotations in a book review.

TABLE OF CONTENTS

1 Introduction 8
    Overview of Honolulu 8
    History 8
    Culture and Diversity 9
    Geography and Landmarks 10
    Economy and Tourism 10
    Lifestyle and Recreation 11
    Conclusion 11

2 Planning your Trip to Honolulu 12
    Best Time to Visit 12
    Entry Requirements and Visa Information 15
    Transportation in Honolulu 18
    Budgeting and Costs for your Trip to Honolulu 33

3 Must-See Attractions 38

Waikiki Beach: Where Paradise Meets the Pacific 38

Diamond Head State Monument: Iconic Crater of Honolulu 43

Pearl Harbor Historic Sites: Honoring History and Valor 49

Hanauma Bay Nature Preserve: Underwater Paradise 54

Iolani Palace: Jewel of Hawaiian Monarchy 59

Bishop Museum: Gateway to Hawaiian and Polynesian Heritage 64

Honolulu Zoo: Where Wildlife Thrives Amidst Tropical Beauty 70

Foster Botanical Garden: A Verdant Paradise in Honolulu 74

4 Outdoor Activities..80

Surfing and Water Sports in Honolulu: Riding the Waves of Aloha......................80

Hiking Trails and Nature Walks in Honolulu: Exploring Nature's Beauty......85

Snorkeling and Diving Spots in Honolulu: Underwater Marvels Await......................90

Whale Watching Tours in Honolulu: Witnessing Nature's Giants......................95

Sunset Cruises in Honolulu: Sailing into Serenity...99

5 Dining and Cuisine 105

Exploring Hawaiian Cuisine: A Fusion of Flavors 105

Best Restaurants and Cafes....................110

Dietary Options and Specialties in Honolulu 115

Food Trucks with Various Options........118

6 Entertainment-Live Music Venues in Honolulu 121

7 Day Trips and Excursions......................126

North Shore Adventure Day Trip 126

Oahu Island Highlights Day Trip...........129

Polynesian Cultural Center Day Trip.....132

Ko Olina Resort Area Day Trip.............135

8 Family-Friendly Activities......................139

Kid-Friendly Attractions on Oahu 139

Family-Oriented Tours on Oahu............144

9 Practical Information 153

Safety Tips for Families Visiting Oahu .153

Local Customs and Etiquette in Hawaii 157

Learning Hawaiian Phrases 159

Emergency Contacts for Oahu...............161

Useful Phrases in Hawaiian 164

BONUS 169

1

INTRODUCTION

OVERVIEW OF HONOLULU

Honolulu, the capital city of Hawaii, stands as a vibrant metropolis juxtaposed against stunning natural beauty. Situated on the island of Oahu, it serves as the political, cultural, and economic heart of Hawaii. Renowned for its inviting climate, pristine beaches, rich history, and diverse culture, Honolulu captivates visitors from around the globe.

HISTORY

The history of Honolulu traces back to ancient Polynesians who settled in the area, followed by European explorers in the 18th century. It gained prominence as a hub for trade and became a strategic military outpost. Later, it was officially established as the capital of the Kingdom of Hawaii by King Kamehameha III in 1850. The city's cultural tapestry is woven from the influences of Native Hawaiian, Asian, and Western traditions.

CULTURE AND DIVERSITY

Honolulu's culture is a vibrant fusion of traditions, showcased through its art, cuisine, festivals, and everyday life. The city celebrates its multicultural identity, with influences from Japan, China, the Philippines, and other Pacific islands blending seamlessly with Hawaiian heritage. Festivals like the Aloha Festivals and Lei Day highlight this rich cultural amalgamation.

GEOGRAPHY AND LANDMARKS

The iconic Diamond Head crater serves as a natural backdrop to the city, while the world-famous Waikiki Beach attracts sun-seekers and surfers alike. Historic sites such as Pearl Harbor, home to the USS Arizona Memorial, stand as a testament to the city's place in world history. Honolulu also boasts lush parks, botanical gardens, and scenic vistas offering panoramic views of the Pacific Ocean.

ECONOMY AND TOURISM

Tourism forms the backbone of Honolulu's economy, drawing millions of visitors annually to its shores. The city's hospitality industry, encompassing luxury resorts, hotels, and a thriving culinary scene, caters to diverse tastes and preferences. Additionally, sectors like military defense, education, and healthcare contribute significantly to its economic landscape.

LIFESTYLE AND RECREATION

Residents and visitors alike revel in Honolulu's outdoor-centric lifestyle. Surfing, snorkeling, hiking, and exploring volcanic landscapes are just a few of the activities available. The city's bustling markets, shopping districts, and dining scene cater to a spectrum of tastes, from local Hawaiian delicacies to international cuisine.

CONCLUSION

Honolulu's allure lies in its ability to seamlessly blend urban sophistication with natural splendor. Its rich cultural heritage, breathtaking landscapes, and warm hospitality create an unforgettable experience for those who explore this captivating city.

2

PLANNING YOUR TRIP TO HONOLULU

BEST TIME TO VISIT

The best time to visit Oahu largely depends on your preferences regarding weather, activities, and crowds. However, generally, the island enjoys pleasant weather throughout the year. Here are some things to think about for various seasons:

High Season (December to March)
Weather: Cooler temperatures, especially in the evenings.

Activities: Ideal for surfing on the North Shore due to higher waves.

Events: Winter months host some festivals and cultural events.

Crowds: Can be crowded due to holiday and winter vacation travelers.

Shoulder Season (April to May, September to November)
Weather: Pleasant temperatures with lower humidity.

Activities: Good for outdoor activities, hiking, and exploring the island.

Crowds: Fewer tourists compared to peak season, but still relatively busy.

Low Season (June to August)
Weather: Warmest months, perfect for beach activities and water sports.

Festivals: Various summer events and festivals occur during these months.

Crowds: Busiest time for tourists, especially families on summer vacation.

Considerations

Surf Conditions: Winter for experienced surfers (North Shore) and calmer waters in summer.

Rates and Accommodation: High season typically has higher rates for hotels and flights.

Humpback Whale Watching: Best in winter (December to March).

Rainfall: Showers are possible year-round but usually brief.

Overall

Year-Round Appeal: Oahu offers attractions and activities throughout the year.

Weather Consistency: Mild and consistent temperatures make it suitable for visits at any time.

Personal Preferences: Consider your preferred activities and tolerance for crowds.

ENTRY REQUIREMENTS AND VISA INFORMATION

Entry requirements for visiting Oahu, which is part of the state of Hawaii, depend on your nationality. Here's an overview:

United States Citizens

No Visa Required: U.S. citizens don't need a visa to visit Hawaii or any other state within the U.S.

Identification: A valid government-issued ID such as a driver's license or passport is required for air travel.

International Visitors

Visa Waiver Program (VWP): Visas are not required for visits lasting up to 90 days for nationals of countries in the Visa Waiver Program.

ESTA Authorization: Travelers under the VWP need to apply for ESTA (Electronic System for Travel Authorization) online before arrival.

Other Visitors

Visa Requirements: Visitors from countries not in the VWP need to apply for a visitor visa (B-2 visa) before traveling to the U.S.

Consult U.S. Embassy or Consulate: Check the specific visa requirements and application process based on your country of citizenship.

COVID-19 Requirements:

Travel Restrictions: Check for any specific COVID-19-related travel restrictions, including testing and quarantine requirements, which may change over time.

Vaccination Proof: Some places might require proof of vaccination or negative COVID-19 test results.

Additional Information

Customs Declaration: Complete a customs declaration form when entering the U.S., declaring items brought into the country.

Length of Stay: Visa and entry requirements might differ based on the intended length of stay, purpose of visit, and individual circumstances.

TRANSPORTATION IN HONOLULU

Transportation in Honolulu offers various options to explore the city and the island of Oahu:

1. Public Transportation

The Bus: Extensive bus system covering most areas of Honolulu and Oahu. Affordable and convenient for getting around the city and to some major attractions.

The Handi-Van: Paratransit service for individuals with disabilities who are unable to use the bus service.

2. Ride-Sharing and Taxis

Uber and Lyft: Readily available and popular for convenient point-to-point transportation.

Taxis: Available throughout the city and commonly found at hotels, malls, and tourist areas.

3. Car Rentals

Car Rental Agencies: Several agencies offer car rentals for travelers who prefer self-guided tours and exploration.

Traffic: Honolulu can have traffic congestion during rush hours, so plan travel times accordingly.

4. Biking and Walking

Bike Rentals: Bike-friendly areas in and around Honolulu; some hotels offer bike rentals.

Pedestrian-Friendly Zones: Areas like Waikiki are pedestrian-friendly, perfect for walking and exploring on foot.

5. Trolley Tours

Hop-on-hop-off trolleys available for tours around Waikiki and to some major attractions. Offers various routes and passes.

6. Shuttles and Tour Services

Shuttle Services: Some hotels offer shuttle services to popular attractions.

Tour Companies: Various tour operators provide transportation for specific tours and activities around the island.

7. Airport Transportation

Shuttles and Taxis: Available at Honolulu International Airport for transportation to hotels and various locations.

Car Rentals: Numerous car rental agencies are located at the airport for convenient access.

Important Considerations:

Parking: Limited parking in certain areas, especially in downtown Honolulu and Waikiki.

Traffic Congestion: Plan for potential traffic, especially during peak hours and near tourist attractions.

Alternative Modes: Embrace walking or biking in pedestrian-friendly areas for a more relaxed exploration.

Accommodation Options

In Honolulu, you'll find a wide range of accommodation options to suit different preferences and budgets:

1. Hotels and Resorts

Luxury Resorts: Iconic beachfront resorts in Waikiki offering amenities like spas, pools, and private beaches. The addresses of some recommended luxury beach resort in Honolulu are given below:

1. Halekulani Hotel

    2199 Kālia Rd, Honolulu, HI 96815

    www.halekulani.com

    +1 808-923-2311

2. Sheraton Waikiki

    2255 Kalākaua Ave, Honolulu, HI 96815

    www.marriott.com

    +1 808-922-4422

3. Hilton Hawaiian Village Waikiki Beach Resort

   2005 Kālia Rd, Honolulu, HI 96815

   www.hilton.com

   +1 808-949-4321

4. Moana Surfrider, Westin Resort and Spa at Waikiki Beach

   2365 Kalākaua Ave, Honolulu, HI 96815

   www.marriott.com

   +1 808-922-3111

5. The Kahala Hotel & Resort

   5000 Kahala Ave, Honolulu, HI 96816

   www.kahalaresort.com

   +1 808-369-9471

Boutique Hotels: Smaller, stylish hotels often with unique themes or designs, offering personalized service. Some boutique hotels include:

1. Vive Hotel Waikiki

    2426 Kūhiō Ave., Honolulu, HI 96815

    www.vivehotelwaikiki.com

    +1 808-687-2000

2. The Equus

    1696 Ala Moana Boulevard, Honolulu, HI 96815

    www.equushotel.com

    +1 808-949-0061

3. Hotel Renew

129 Paoakalani Ave, Honolulu, HI 96815

www.hotelrenew.com

+1 808-687-7700

4. The Beach Waikiki Boutique Hostel by ALOH

2569 Cartwright Rd, Honolulu, HI 96815

www.thebeachwaikikihostel.com

5. Paradise Bay Resort Hawaii

47-039 Lihikai Dr, Kaneohe, HI 96744

www.paradisebayresort.com

+1 808-239-5711

Business Hotels: Conveniently located near business districts and offer business-oriented amenities. Our recommended business hotels are listed below:

1. Hotel La Croix

   2070 Kalākaua Ave, Honolulu, HI 96815

   www.lacroixwaikiki.com

   +1 808-942-6060

2. Prince Waikiki

   00 Holomoana St, Honolulu, HI 96815

   www.princewaikiki.com

   +1 855-622-7558

3. Outrigger Reef Waikiki Beach Resort

   2169 Kālia Rd, Honolulu, HI 96815

www.outrigger.com

+1 866-956-4262

4. Hotel Renew

129 Paoakalani Ave, Honolulu, HI 96815

www.hotelrenew.com

+1 808-687-7700

5. Hyatt Place Waikiki Beach

175 Paoakalani Ave, Honolulu, HI 96815

www.hyatt.com

+1 808-922-3861

2. Vacation Rentals

Condos and Apartments: Renting a condo or apartment can provide a more private and home-like atmosphere for families or longer stays.

Vacation Homes: Ideal for larger groups, providing more space and privacy, often located in residential areas.

3. Hostels and Budget Accommodations

Hostels: Budget-friendly options, offering dormitory-style rooms or private rooms with shared facilities.

Budget Hotels and Motels: Affordable accommodations with basic amenities, suitable for travelers on a budget. Our recommended accommodations under this category are given below:

1. Polynesian Hostel Beach Club

2584 Lemon Rd, Honolulu, HI 96815

www.polynesianhostel.com

+1 808-922-1340

2. HI Honolulu University Hostel

2323A Seaview Ave, Honolulu, HI 96822

www.hostelsaloha.com

+1 808-946-0591

3. Seaside Hawaiian Hostel

419 Seaside Ave, Honolulu, HI 96815

www.seasidehawaiianhostel.com

+1 808-453-0446

4. Waikiki Beachside Hostel

2552 Lemon Rd, Honolulu, HI 96815

www.waikikibeachsidehostel.com

+1 808-923-9566

5. Pacific Ohana Hostel

2566 Lemon Rd, Honolulu, HI 96815

www.hawaiihostelwaikiki.com

+1 808-921-8111

4. Bed and Breakfasts

B&Bs are often found outside the main city, offering cozy rooms and personalized service, sometimes with homemade breakfast included.

5. Luxury Rentals and Villas

High-end private rentals or villas offering luxury amenities, privacy, and personalized services.

6. Extended Stay Accommodations

Extended Stay Hotels: Designed for longer stays, offering amenities like kitchens and laundry facilities.

Corporate Housing: Furnished apartments or homes tailored for business travelers or longer-term stays.

7. Eco-Friendly and Sustainable Lodging

Eco-Resorts: Accommodations focused on sustainability and eco-friendly practices, offering unique experiences.

Considerations:

Location: Decide if you prefer beachfront, downtown, or quieter areas.

Amenities: Prioritize amenities such as pools, spas, fitness centers, or family-friendly facilities.

Budget: Determine your budget range and choose accordingly.

Reviews and Ratings: Check online reviews to ensure the accommodation meets your expectations.

BUDGETING AND COSTS FOR YOUR TRIP TO HONOLULU

Budgeting for a trip to Honolulu involves considering various expenses, including accommodation, transportation, food, activities, and miscellaneous costs. Here's a breakdown to help plan your budget:

Accommodation

Budget: Hostels, budget hotels, or vacation rentals can range from $100-$300 per night.

Mid-Range: Boutique hotels or standard hotels can range from $200-$350 per night.

Luxury: Beachfront resorts or high-end accommodations can exceed $300 per night.

Transportation

Car Rentals: Daily rates vary but can range from $40-$100 per day, depending on the type of vehicle and rental agency.

Public Transportation: Bus fares are around $2.75 per ride, and day passes are available for approximately $5.50.

Food and Dining

Budget: Meals at local eateries or food trucks can range from $10-$20 per person.

Mid-Range: Restaurants or casual dining might cost $20-$40 per person.

Fine Dining: Upscale restaurants can cost $50 and above per person for a meal.

Activities and Attractions

Tours and Excursions: Prices vary but can range from $50-$200 per person for guided tours or activities.

Museums and Parks: Entrance fees to attractions can vary but often range from $10-$30 per person.

Miscellaneous

Shopping: Souvenirs, clothing, or local products can add to your expenses.

Tips and Gratuities: Tipping for services is customary and should be factored into your budget.

Emergency Funds: Allocate some funds for unforeseen expenses or emergencies.

Overall Tips

Advance Booking: Booking accommodations and flights in advance can sometimes lead to better deals.

Off-Peak Travel: Traveling during shoulder seasons might offer lower rates and fewer crowds.

Budget-Friendly Options: Opt for free or low-cost activities like beach visits or hiking.

Summary

Daily Budget: Depending on your lifestyle and preferences, a daily budget can range from $150-$300 per person (excluding accommodation).

Total Trip Budget: For a week-long trip, a rough estimate could be $1500-$3000 per person, considering accommodation, transportation, food, and activities.

Remember

Create a detailed budget outline considering your preferences, group size, and desired activities.

Consider additional costs like travel insurance, souvenirs, and unexpected expenses.

Disclaimer

Costs can vary widely based on personal choices, preferences, travel style, and currency fluctuations. Always research and plan based on your specific needs and circumstances.

3

MUST-SEE ATTRACTIONS

WAIKIKI BEACH: WHERE PARADISE MEETS THE PACIFIC

Waikiki Beach stands as an iconic destination synonymous with sun-kissed shores, azure waters, and a vibrant atmosphere. Nestled along the southern shore of Oahu, this world-renowned beach is not just a location; it's a sensation, an experience that captures the essence of Hawaii's allure.

A Brief History

Once a playground for Hawaiian royalty, Waikiki evolved from a serene retreat to a bustling hub for travelers from around the globe. Its transformation from a retreat for

Hawaiian nobility to a sought-after tourist destination mirrors the growth of Hawaii's tourism industry.

The Beach Experience

1. Golden Sands and Azure Waters

Waikiki's two-mile stretch of pristine shoreline offers golden sands that invite visitors to relax under the Hawaiian sun. The gentle waves of the Pacific Ocean create ideal conditions for swimming, surfing, and various water sports.

2. Diamond Head Backdrop

The iconic silhouette of Diamond Head Crater provides a breathtaking backdrop, adding to the beach's visual splendor. A hike to the summit of Diamond Head offers panoramic views of Waikiki Beach and the surrounding landscape.

Attractions Along the Shoreline

1. Duke Kahanamoku Statue

Honoring the legendary surfer and Olympic swimmer, Duke Kahanamoku, this statue stands as a tribute to his legacy. A popular spot for photos and a reminder of Hawaii's surfing heritage.

2. Kapiolani Park

Adjacent to Waikiki, this lush park offers a serene retreat from the bustling beach scene.

Features include jogging paths, gardens, and the Honolulu Zoo.

Activities and Entertainment

1. Surfing Lessons

Embrace the spirit of the ocean by taking surf lessons from seasoned instructors.

Waikiki's gentle waves are perfect for beginners looking to catch their first wave.

2. Catamaran and Sunset Cruises

Sail on a catamaran to witness breathtaking views of the coastline and Diamond Head at sunset. Enjoy cocktails and live music aboard these relaxing cruises.

Shopping and Dining

1. Kalakaua Avenue

The bustling thoroughfare adjacent to Waikiki Beach offers a myriad of shops, boutiques, and upscale retailers. Explore a variety of dining options ranging from fine dining to casual beachside eateries.

2. International Marketplace

A bustling marketplace housing an array of shops, artisan stalls, and restaurants.

Find unique souvenirs, local crafts, and indulge in diverse cuisines.

Events and Festivities

1. Waikiki Hula Show

Complimentary hula shows held at Kuhio Beach Park offer a glimpse into Hawaiian culture and dance. Traditional performances featuring skilled hula dancers captivate audiences.

2. Annual Festivals

Events like the Waikiki Spam Jam and Waikiki Hoolaulea celebrate Hawaiian culture through music, food, and entertainment.

Conclusion

Waikiki Beach embodies the essence of Hawaii's natural beauty, cultural richness, and vibrant energy. It's not merely a beach; it's a destination that captivates the senses, offering a blend of relaxation, adventure, and cultural immersion. From leisurely strolls along the shoreline to thrilling water activities and vibrant nightlife, Waikiki Beach ensures an unforgettable experience that resonates long after the sand is brushed off. In its embrace, visitors discover the magic that has drawn travelers to this slice of paradise for generations.

DIAMOND HEAD STATE MONUMENT: ICONIC CRATER OF HONOLULU

Introduction

Diamond Head State Monument stands as an iconic symbol overlooking Honolulu, a volcanic tuff cone that has become synonymous with the stunning landscapes of

Oahu, Hawaii. This geological marvel offers not just a hike but an expedition through history and breathtaking vistas.

Historical Significance

1. Ancient Origins

Formed over 300,000 years ago from a volcanic eruption, Diamond Head, known as Le'ahi in Hawaiian, served as a prominent landmark for early seafarers. Hawaiians used the crater as a navigational aid and for military purposes.

2. Military Outpost

In the early 20th century, the U.S. military utilized Diamond Head as a strategic coastal defense site, evident in the fortifications and bunkers. The location played a crucial role during World War II, serving as a lookout and defense post.

The Hiking Experience

1. Trail Overview

The hike begins with a moderate ascent, leading through tunnels and up staircases carved into the crater's interior. Approximately 0.8 miles (1.3 km) each way, the trail rewards hikers with panoramic views.

2. Summit Ascent

The final ascent to the summit involves a series of steep stairs and narrow passageways, culminating in an awe-inspiring view. Visitors are greeted with sweeping vistas of Waikiki Beach, Honolulu, and the Pacific Ocean.

Spectacular Views

1. Overlooking Waikiki

The vantage point from the summit showcases Waikiki's skyline, the expansive Pacific, and the turquoise hues of the shoreline. The contrasting urban landscape against the natural beauty of the coastline creates a mesmerizing sight.

2. Diamond Head Crater Panorama

Lookout points along the trail offer glimpses into the crater's interior, revealing its geological formations and lush vegetation. Photographers flock to capture the unique perspectives of Diamond Head's slopes and the crater floor.

Tips and Practical Information

1. Preparation

Wear comfortable hiking shoes and bring water, sunscreen, and a hat, as the trail has minimal shade. To avoid crowds and take advantage of the cooler weather, come early.

2. Accessibility

While the hike is moderately challenging, it's accessible to most fitness levels. Visitors should note that parts of the trail involve uneven terrain and steep ascents.

Environmental Conservation

1. Preservation Efforts

Diamond Head State Monument is protected and managed to preserve its natural and historical significance. Visitors are encouraged to adhere to trail etiquette and respect the environment.

2. Educational Significance

Educational signage along the trail provides insights into the geological formations, flora, and fauna of the area. Visitors gain a deeper understanding of the crater's ecological importance.

Conclusion

Diamond Head State Monument is more than a geological wonder; it's a testament to Hawaii's rich history, geological forces, and natural beauty. The hike to its summit offers not only breathtaking views but also a journey through time, providing a glimpse into the past and a deep appreciation for the island's diverse landscapes. As visitors ascend its slopes and reach the pinnacle, they're rewarded with a panoramic spectacle that encapsulates the magic of Oahu, leaving an indelible mark on their memories.

PEARL HARBOR HISTORIC SITES: HONORING HISTORY AND VALOR

Introduction

Pearl Harbor stands as a poignant symbol of American history, where a pivotal moment changed the course of a nation and the world. This harbor, forever etched in history, serves as a memorial to those who lost their lives on December 7, 1941, and a testament to the bravery and sacrifice of countless individuals.

Historical Significance

1. The Attack

The United States entered World War II as a result of a surprise aerial attack by the Japanese Imperial Navy on the U.S. Pacific Fleet, which was based at Pearl Harbor, on December 7, 1941. The attack left a devastating impact, destroying battleships and claiming the lives of over 2,400 service members and civilians.

2. World War II Valor in the Pacific National Monument

The historic sites within Pearl Harbor, including the USS Arizona Memorial, USS Missouri, USS Bowfin Submarine, and Pacific Aviation Museum, are part of the World War II Valor in the Pacific National Monument. Each site provides a unique perspective on the events of that fateful day and the ensuing war.

Key Attractions

1. USS Arizona Memorial

Suspended over the sunken battleship USS Arizona, this memorial honors the 1,177 crew members who perished during the attack.

Visitors take a solemn boat ride to the memorial, reflecting on the sacrifices made in the defense of freedom.

2. USS Missouri

Known as the "Mighty Mo," this battleship served in World War II, hosting the Japanese surrender ceremony in 1945, marking the end of the war. Guided tours allow visitors to explore the ship and learn about its storied past.

3. USS Bowfin Submarine Museum

The USS Bowfin, a World War II submarine nicknamed the "Pearl Harbor Avenger," offers a glimpse into life aboard a submarine during wartime. The museum showcases artifacts and exhibits detailing submarine operations.

4. Pacific Aviation Museum

Housed in historic hangars that survived the attack, the museum displays aircraft and exhibits chronicling aviation history in the Pacific. Interactive displays and educational programs engage visitors in the evolution of aviation.

The Experience

1. Commemoration and Reflection

Visiting Pearl Harbor is a solemn and reflective experience, offering a chance to pay respects to the fallen and learn about the bravery and resilience of those involved. Educational programs and guided tours provide historical context and personal stories of heroism.

2. Educational Significance

Interpretive exhibits, films, and memorabilia at each site offer insights into the events leading up to the attack and its aftermath.

The sites serve as educational tools to ensure the memory of the sacrifice endures for future generations.

Conclusion

Pearl Harbor's historic sites serve as a testament to the resilience of a nation and the valor of its servicemen and women. As visitors explore these hallowed grounds, they're immersed in a journey through history, gaining a profound understanding of the impact of war and the significance of remembrance. The experience leaves an indelible mark, fostering a deep appreciation for the sacrifices made and the enduring spirit of honor and courage that defines the legacy of Pearl Harbor.

HANAUMA BAY NATURE PRESERVE: UNDERWATER PARADISE

Introduction

Nestled within a volcanic crater on the southeastern coast of Oahu, Hanauma Bay Nature Preserve is a marine paradise renowned for its crystal-clear waters, vibrant coral reefs, and diverse marine life. This natural treasure offers visitors an immersive experience into Hawaii's underwater world.

Ecological Significance

1. Marine Conservation Area

Designated as a protected marine conservation area in 1967, Hanauma Bay is a sanctuary for over 400 species of fish and various marine creatures. The preservation efforts aim to conserve the delicate coral reefs and ecosystem.

2. Coral Reef Restoration

Ongoing conservation initiatives include coral reef restoration projects aimed at preserving and rehabilitating the delicate coral formations. These efforts are crucial in sustaining the biodiversity of the bay's marine life.

Visitor Experience

1. Snorkeling and Diving

Snorkeling at Hanauma Bay offers a mesmerizing glimpse into an underwater world teeming with colorful fish, sea turtles, and vibrant coral. The calm, shallow waters make it an ideal spot for both beginners and experienced snorkelers.

2. Educational Programs

Visitor Center: Offers educational exhibits, presentations, and videos detailing the bay's ecology, marine life, and conservation efforts.

Snorkeling etiquette and safety guidelines are emphasized to protect the fragile ecosystem.

Key Attractions

1. Marine Life

Encounter an array of marine species, including parrotfish, butterflyfish, surgeonfish, and the occasional green sea turtle. The vibrant colors and diversity of fish species create a captivating underwater spectacle.

2. Hiking Trails and Scenic Views

Scenic hiking trails around the rim of the crater offer panoramic views of the bay and the surrounding coastline.

Visitors can appreciate the bay's beauty from a different perspective while taking in the lush coastal landscapes.

Practical Information

1. Entry Requirements and Fees

Visitors are required to watch an educational video at the Visitor Center, outlining conservation guidelines, before entering the bay. Entry fees help fund conservation efforts and maintaining the preserve.

2. Sustainable Tourism Practices

To protect the bay's fragile ecosystem, visitors are encouraged to use reef-safe sunscreen, refrain from touching or stepping on corals, and avoid feeding marine life.

The Hanauma Bay Experience

1. Tranquility and Natural Beauty

Beyond its ecological importance, Hanauma Bay offers a serene setting where visitors can connect with nature and find tranquility by the sea. The bay's picturesque landscapes and tranquil waters create an idyllic atmosphere.

2. Conservation Awareness

Visitors depart with a deeper appreciation for marine conservation efforts and the importance of responsible tourism. The experience fosters a sense of stewardship toward preserving natural wonders for future generations.

Conclusion

Hanauma Bay Nature Preserve is a testament to Hawaii's natural beauty and the delicate balance of its marine ecosystems. Visitors embarking on a journey to this aquatic wonderland not only immerse themselves in a vibrant underwater world but also gain a profound appreciation for the importance of preserving fragile environments. The bay's allure extends beyond its scenic beauty, leaving visitors with a sense of reverence for nature's wonders and the responsibility to protect these invaluable treasures.

IOLANI PALACE: JEWEL OF HAWAIIAN MONARCHY

Introduction

Iolani Palace, nestled in downtown Honolulu, serves as a captivating testament to Hawaii's royal legacy and cultural heritage. As the only royal palace in the United States, it stands as a revered symbol of the Hawaiian monarchy's grandeur and the island nation's history.

Historical Significance

1. Royal Residence

Completed in 1882, Iolani Palace served as the official residence of Hawaii's last reigning monarchs, King Kalakaua and Queen Liliuokalani. The palace witnessed both the lavish festivities of the Hawaiian monarchy and the tumultuous transition to a republic.

2. Overthrow and Annexation

The palace bore witness to the 1893 overthrow of Queen Liliuokalani by American businessmen and the subsequent annexation of Hawaii by the United States. This pivotal moment in history marked the end of Hawaii's sovereign rule and the dawn of a new era.

Architectural Marvel

1. Intricate Design

Iolani Palace boasts a unique architectural blend of Hawaiian and Western influences, featuring ornate Victorian-style architecture combined with traditional Hawaiian motifs. The intricate woodwork, elegant interiors, and opulent décor reflect the grandeur of the monarchy.

2. Royal Grounds

The palace grounds encompass beautifully landscaped gardens, including the Coronation Pavilion where Hawaiian monarchs were crowned. The grand staircase and intricate ironwork gates add to the palace's regal charm.

Visitor Experience

1. Palace Tours

Guided tours offer a glimpse into the royal past, showcasing the opulent Throne Room, State Dining Room, private suites, and the queen's music room. Visitors gain insights into the monarchy's cultural significance and the palace's role in Hawaiian history.

2. Cultural Enrichment

Cultural programs and exhibits highlight Hawaiian history, traditions, and the monarchy's legacy. Live performances and educational presentations provide deeper insights into the rich heritage of Hawaii's indigenous culture.

Preservation and Restoration

1. Restoration Efforts

Extensive restoration work has preserved the palace's original grandeur, ensuring its historical integrity remains intact. Restoration projects aim to conserve artifacts, furnishings, and the palace's architectural authenticity.

2. Educational Significance

Iolani Palace serves as an educational hub, fostering awareness of Hawaii's royal heritage and its significance in American history.

Educational programs cater to visitors of all ages, offering immersive experiences into Hawaiian culture and history.

Conclusion

Iolani Palace stands not only as an architectural marvel but as a living testament to Hawaii's royal legacy and the resilience of its people. As visitors step through its grand halls and lush gardens, they're transported back in time to an era of regal splendor and cultural richness. The palace's historical significance and its role in shaping Hawaii's identity make it a cherished heritage site, inviting visitors to immerse themselves in the captivating story of the Hawaiian monarchy and its enduring legacy.

BISHOP MUSEUM: GATEWAY TO HAWAIIAN AND POLYNESIAN HERITAGE

Introduction

The Bishop Museum, situated in Honolulu, stands as a beacon of Hawaiian and Polynesian heritage, preserving and celebrating the cultural legacy of the Pacific region. Founded in 1889, it serves as a repository of artifacts, historical records, and scientific research, offering a glimpse into the diverse cultures of Hawaii and the Pacific.

Historical Significance

1. Legacy of Charles Reed Bishop

Founded by Charles Reed Bishop in honor of his late wife, Princess Bernice Pauahi Bishop, the museum serves as a tribute to her commitment to education and Hawaiian culture. Princess Bernice Pauahi Bishop was a descendant of the Hawaiian royal family and a prominent philanthropist.

2. Preservation of Culture

The museum's mission revolves around preserving, perpetuating, and interpreting the cultural and natural history of Hawaii and the Pacific Islands.

It houses one of the world's most extensive collections of Polynesian artifacts and cultural treasures.

Key Exhibits and Collections

1. Hawaiian Hall

Divided into three main galleries, Hawaiian Hall showcases artifacts, traditional crafts, tools, and exhibits that narrate the history and customs of the Hawaiian people. Visitors encounter displays depicting Hawaiian mythology, rituals, and the daily lives of ancient Hawaiians.

2. Pacific Hall

Explores the diverse cultures of Polynesia, Melanesia, and Micronesia through interactive exhibits, artworks, and artifacts.

Offers insights into the unique traditions, languages, and lifestyles of various Pacific Island cultures.

Visitor Experience

1. Cultural Enrichment

Engaging programs, demonstrations, and presentations provide visitors with a deeper understanding of Hawaiian and Pacific Island cultures. Live performances, storytelling, and educational workshops showcase traditional practices and arts.

2. Planetarium and Science Adventure Center

The planetarium offers immersive celestial experiences, while the Science Adventure Center features interactive exhibits focused on natural history and scientific exploration.

Visitors can engage in hands-on activities and delve into topics like volcanology, biodiversity, and astronomy.

Educational Outreach and Research

1. Research Initiatives

The museum houses extensive research facilities, including collections, archives, and laboratories dedicated to scientific exploration and cultural preservation. Ongoing research contributes to the understanding of Pacific history, natural sciences, and cultural anthropology.

2. Educational Programs

Educational outreach programs cater to schools, educators, and learners of all ages, offering curriculum-based resources and immersive learning experiences.

Workshops, field trips, and digital resources aim to foster a deeper appreciation for Pacific heritage and scientific discovery.

Conclusion

The Bishop Museum stands as a custodian of Hawaii's cultural heritage and a gateway to the vast Pacific region's diversity. Its immersive exhibits, educational programs, and commitment to research offer visitors a multifaceted exploration of Hawaiian and Polynesian cultures. As visitors traverse its galleries and engage in interactive experiences, they embark on a journey through time and space, gaining a profound appreciation for the rich tapestry of traditions, history, and scientific wonders that define the Pacific region.

HONOLULU ZOO: WHERE WILDLIFE THRIVES AMIDST TROPICAL BEAUTY

Introduction

Nestled in the heart of Waikiki, the Honolulu Zoo beckons visitors into a world of diverse wildlife, tropical flora, and educational exhibits. Established in 1914, the zoo stands as a testament to Hawaii's commitment to conservation and animal welfare.

Wildlife and Habitats

1. Species Diversity

The zoo houses over 900 animals, representing a wide array of species from around the globe, including mammals, birds, reptiles, and amphibians. Visitors encounter endangered species like Sumatran tigers, Komodo dragons, and several rare bird species.

2. Habitat Diversity

Habitats replicate natural environments, including tropical rainforests, savannas, and aquatic ecosystems, allowing animals to thrive in environments akin to their natural habitats. Themed exhibits create immersive experiences, such as the African Savannah and the Pacific Islands section.

Educational and Conservation Efforts

1. Conservation Initiatives

The zoo actively participates in wildlife conservation programs, focusing on species preservation and habitat protection.

Educational programs and exhibits raise awareness about endangered species and conservation challenges.

2. Educational Programs

The zoo offers educational workshops, guided tours, and interactive programs for visitors of all ages. School programs cater to curriculum-based learning, fostering an appreciation for wildlife and environmental stewardship.

Visitor Experience

1. Animal Encounters

Visitors have the opportunity to observe and learn about a diverse range of animals through scheduled feeding sessions, keeper talks, and animal enrichment activities. Animal encounters provide engaging and educational experiences for visitors.

2. Lush Landscapes

The zoo's scenic setting amidst lush tropical landscapes offers a serene escape from the urban bustle of Waikiki. Beautiful gardens, ponds, and shaded pathways enhance the visitor experience.

Family-Friendly Features

1. Keiki Zoo

Designed for younger visitors, the Keiki Zoo offers hands-on activities, interactive exhibits, and a petting zoo. Children can learn about animals through play and exploration.

2. Conservation Plaza

An educational area focusing on conservation efforts, showcasing innovative initiatives and inspiring visitors to take action toward environmental sustainability. Interactive exhibits engage visitors in understanding conservation challenges and solutions.

Conclusion

The Honolulu Zoo serves as a haven for wildlife enthusiasts, nature lovers, and families seeking an immersive encounter with the animal kingdom. Its commitment to conservation, diverse range of species, and engaging educational programs create an environment where visitors not only appreciate the beauty of nature but also gain a deeper understanding of the importance of wildlife conservation. As visitors wander through its lush landscapes and encounter fascinating creatures, they embark on a journey of discovery and appreciation for the marvels of the natural world.

FOSTER BOTANICAL GARDEN: A VERDANT PARADISE IN HONOLULU

Introduction

Established in 1853, Foster Botanical Garden stands as one of the oldest botanical gardens in Hawaii, showcasing a diverse collection of tropical plants and offering a serene escape within the bustling city of Honolulu.

Botanical Diversity

1. Tropical Plant Collections

The garden spans over 14 acres, featuring a vast array of tropical plants, rare trees, and exotic flowers from various regions, including the South Pacific, India, Sri Lanka, and the Americas. Visitors encounter diverse ecosystems, from rainforest species to arid desert plants, creating a tapestry of botanical wonders.

2. Historic Trees

Some of the garden's iconic features include its collection of historic trees, including the magnificent Indian banyan tree, which spreads its sprawling canopy over a significant area.

The Exceptional Trees program highlights and conserves significant trees on the island, showcasing their historical and botanical importance.

Gardens and Landscapes

1. Themed Gardens

Foster Botanical Garden boasts themed gardens, such as the Economic Garden featuring plants of economic importance, the Prehistoric Glen with ancient plant species, and the Butterfly Garden attracting local species. Each garden provides a unique experience, blending beauty with educational value.

2. Orchid Display

The Orchid Conservatory showcases a stunning collection of orchids, renowned for their vibrant colors, intricate shapes, and captivating fragrances. Visitors marvel at the variety of orchid species on display, representing some of the world's most exquisite blooms.

Visitor Experience

1. Guided Tours and Educational Programs

Knowledgeable guides offer insights into the garden's history, plant collections, and conservation efforts through guided tours and educational programs. School programs and workshops cater to students and educators, fostering an appreciation for plant diversity and conservation.

2. Tranquil Settings

Visitors can explore serene pathways, serene ponds, and shaded areas, providing tranquil spots for relaxation and contemplation amidst the botanical splendor. Benches and gazebos scattered throughout the garden offer ideal spots to immerse in nature's beauty.

Conservation and Preservation

1. Plant Conservation Efforts

The garden participates in plant conservation initiatives, preserving endangered species and supporting plant research and propagation. Efforts focus on conserving rare and threatened plant species, contributing to global biodiversity efforts.

2. Educational Significance

Foster Botanical Garden serves as an educational resource for botanical studies, research, and public outreach, fostering awareness about tropical plant diversity and conservation. Interpretive signage and educational materials provide valuable information to visitors about the garden's plant collections and significance.

Conclusion

Foster Botanical Garden is a botanical paradise that captivates visitors with its vibrant plant collections, serene landscapes, and educational experiences. As visitors wander through its diverse gardens and encounter rare and exotic flora, they not only appreciate the beauty of tropical plants but also gain a deeper understanding of the importance of preserving and conserving botanical diversity. The garden's tranquil ambiance and rich botanical heritage offer a sanctuary for nature enthusiasts, inviting them to explore, learn, and connect with the wonders of the plant kingdom.

4

OUTDOOR ACTIVITIES

SURFING AND WATER SPORTS IN HONOLULU: RIDING THE WAVES OF ALOHA

Surfing Culture

1. Legendary Surfing Legacy

Hawaii is the birthplace of surfing, and the sport holds a significant place in Hawaiian culture, dating back centuries. Surfing embodies the spirit of aloha, emphasizing respect for the ocean and its waves.

2. Iconic Surf Spots

Waikiki Beach, with its gentle rolling waves, is a renowned destination for beginner surfers to catch their first rides and learn the art of surfing. Bigger waves at spots like Diamond Head and Ala Moana Bowls attract more experienced surfers seeking thrilling rides.

Water Sports Extravaganza

1. Stand-Up Paddleboarding (SUP)

Honolulu's calm waters make it ideal for stand-up paddleboarding, offering a unique way to explore the coastline while enjoying a full-body workout. SUP enthusiasts can paddle along Waikiki Beach or venture into quieter bays and inlets.

2. Snorkeling and Diving

Hanauma Bay Nature Preserve offers an exceptional snorkeling experience, allowing visitors to explore vibrant coral reefs and encounter diverse marine life.

Diving enthusiasts can explore shipwrecks, caves, and underwater formations teeming with marine biodiversity.

Surf Schools and Lessons

1. Surfing Lessons

Numerous surf schools and instructors along Waikiki Beach offer lessons catering to all skill levels, from beginners to advanced surfers. Expert instructors provide guidance on paddling, catching waves, and maintaining proper surfing etiquette.

2. Water Safety

Water safety is paramount, and beginners are encouraged to learn from certified instructors who prioritize safety and respect for the ocean. Understanding wave patterns, currents, and beach safety guidelines is crucial for an enjoyable experience.

Thriving Water Culture

1. Surf Competitions and Events

Honolulu hosts various surfing competitions, attracting local talent and international surfers. Events celebrate the sport's heritage and showcase the prowess of surfers riding Hawaii's legendary waves.

2. Water-Based Adventures

Beyond surfing, visitors can indulge in a myriad of water-based adventures, including jet skiing, parasailing, and kayak tours along the coastline. Sunset catamaran cruises offer a relaxing way to witness breathtaking views of the Pacific while enjoying the ocean breeze.

Conclusion

Honolulu's vibrant water sports scene offers a blend of tradition, adventure, and excitement. From the ancient art of surfing to modern-day water activities, the city's stunning coastline beckons enthusiasts of all ages and skill levels. Embracing the spirit of aloha, water sports in Honolulu not only provide exhilarating experiences but also foster a deep connection with the ocean, its waves, and the cultural heritage that has made surfing an integral part of Hawaiian identity. Whether catching waves, exploring underwater marvels, or embarking on aquatic adventures, Honolulu's waters invite visitors to dive in and ride the waves of aloha.

HIKING TRAILS AND NATURE WALKS IN HONOLULU: EXPLORING NATURE'S BEAUTY

Diverse Trail Experiences

1. Diamond Head Summit Trail

Offering panoramic views of Waikiki and the southeastern coastline, this iconic hike takes visitors through historic military bunkers and tunnels to the summit of Diamond Head Crater. Moderate difficulty, with well-maintained pathways and stairs leading to breathtaking vistas.

2. Manoa Falls Trail

Located in a lush rainforest valley, this trail leads to the majestic Manoa Falls, a 150-foot waterfall surrounded by verdant foliage.

A relatively easy hike, perfect for families and nature enthusiasts, showcasing the beauty of Hawaii's tropical forests.

Coastal Beauty

1. Makapuu Lighthouse Trail

Overlooking the scenic coastline, this trail offers stunning vistas of the Pacific Ocean and the Makapuu Lighthouse. An accessible paved path, perfect for whale watching during the winter months and admiring coastal landscapes.

2. Kaena Point Trail

Located on Oahu's westernmost tip, this coastal trail provides a unique opportunity to explore rugged shoreline, tide pools, and seabird sanctuaries.

A remote and scenic hike, showcasing natural beauty and offering a chance to spot Hawaiian monk seals and seabirds.

Rainforest Escapes

1. Aiea Loop Trail

Winding through lush rainforest and offering glimpses of Pearl Harbor, this moderate loop trail features shaded pathways and scenic lookout points. A favorite among hikers for its diverse flora and peaceful ambiance.

2. Lyon Arboretum

Home to a variety of botanical collections, this garden sanctuary offers several trails winding through diverse tropical landscapes. Visitors can explore themed gardens, exotic plant species, and learn about Hawaii's native flora.

Practical Tips

1. Preparedness

Wear sturdy footwear, carry water, sunscreen, insect repellent, and dress in layers as weather conditions can vary. Check trail conditions and heed posted signs for safety.

2. Respect for Nature

Practice Leave No Trace principles, respecting wildlife, plants, and the environment. Stay on designated trails to preserve the natural habitat and avoid disturbing sensitive ecosystems.

Enjoying Nature's Bounty

1. Wildlife Encounters

Hiking trails offer opportunities to spot native birds, insects, and sometimes endangered species, providing an immersive experience in Hawaii's natural world. Look out for wildlife while respecting their natural habitats.

2. Sunrise and Sunset Views

Many trails offer spectacular sunrise and sunset views, creating unforgettable experiences amidst nature's beauty. Capture breathtaking moments while embracing the tranquility of the landscape.

Conclusion

Honolulu's hiking trails and nature walks offer a diverse tapestry of landscapes, from lush rainforests to coastal vistas, providing nature enthusiasts with a range of experiences. Whether admiring cascading waterfalls, exploring rainforest trails, or gazing at panoramic coastal views, each hike offers a chance to immerse in the beauty of Hawaii's natural wonders. With trails suitable for various skill levels and interests, visitors can embark on an adventure through Honolulu's scenic landscapes, connecting with nature and discovering the island's hidden treasures.

SNORKELING AND DIVING SPOTS IN HONOLULU: UNDERWATER MARVELS AWAIT

Hanauma Bay Nature Preserve

1. Snorkeling Paradise

Hanauma Bay offers a spectacular snorkeling experience, featuring a protected marine ecosystem with clear waters, vibrant coral reefs, and diverse marine species. Visitors can encounter colorful fish, sea turtles, and fascinating reef formations within the bay's calm and shallow waters.

2. Educational Opportunity

The bay's visitor center provides educational resources and safety guidelines, ensuring a memorable and responsible snorkeling experience. A must-visit spot for snorkelers of all skill levels seeking to explore Hawaii's underwater beauty.

Waikiki Beach

1. Beginner-Friendly Snorkeling

Waikiki's gentle waves make it an ideal spot for beginners to snorkel and explore nearshore reefs. The reef areas host an array of tropical fish species and occasional sightings of sea turtles.

2. Close to Amenities

Snorkeling at Waikiki Beach offers the convenience of nearby amenities, making it easily accessible for families and novice snorkelers.

Oahu's South Shore

1. Diving Hotspots

Oahu's South Shore boasts diverse diving sites catering to both novice and experienced divers. Sites like Kewalo Pipe, Turtle Canyons, and the Sea Tiger shipwreck offer encounters with sea turtles, colorful marine life, and captivating underwater structures.

2. Wreck Diving

The Sea Tiger, a sunken ship, provides an opportunity for wreck diving, allowing divers to explore a unique artificial reef teeming with marine creatures.

Electric Beach (Kahe Point Beach Park)

1. Rich Marine Life

Known for its warm water currents, Electric Beach offers exceptional snorkeling and diving experiences with abundant marine life. Visitors can witness sea turtles, dolphins, and schools of tropical fish attracted to the warm water outflow from a nearby power plant.

2. Advanced Diving Opportunities

Divers can explore deeper waters near the power plant's outflow, encountering larger marine species and unique underwater landscapes.

Safety Tips

1. Snorkeling and Diving Etiquette

Respect marine life and refrain from touching or disturbing coral reefs and wildlife. Practice proper snorkeling and diving techniques, and use reef-safe sunscreen to protect the delicate underwater ecosystem.

2. Safety Precautions

Check weather conditions and follow safety guidelines before snorkeling or diving.

Use well-maintained equipment and consider guided tours for a safer and more enriching experience.

Conclusion

Honolulu's snorkeling and diving spots offer a gateway to a mesmerizing underwater world. From the protected marine sanctuary of Hanauma Bay to the diverse diving sites along Oahu's South Shore, each spot provides an opportunity to witness the beauty and diversity of Hawaii's marine ecosystems. Whether exploring vibrant coral reefs, encountering sea turtles, or venturing into deeper waters, these snorkeling and diving spots promise unforgettable experiences for water enthusiasts seeking to immerse themselves in the splendor of Honolulu's aquatic wonders.

WHALE WATCHING TOURS IN HONOLULU: WITNESSING NATURE'S GIANTS

Seasonal Migration

1. Winter Spectacle

Humpback whales migrate to Hawaii's warm waters during the winter months, typically from December to April, seeking breeding and calving grounds. This migration brings thousands of these magnificent creatures to the Hawaiian islands.

2. Prime Viewing Season

Peak whale watching season in Honolulu typically occurs between January and March when sightings of humpback whales are most frequent and reliable. Whale watching tours during this time offer an opportunity to witness these giants up close.

Tour Experiences

1. Guided Excursions

Several tour operators in Honolulu offer guided whale watching excursions, providing knowledgeable guides and captains who are familiar with whale behavior and migration patterns. Tours range from catamaran cruises to smaller boat expeditions, catering to different preferences.

2. Educational Insights

Expert guides on these tours share insights into humpback whale behavior, biology, and conservation efforts, enhancing the educational aspect of the experience. Visitors learn about the whales' unique behaviors, such as breaching, tail slapping, and singing.

Ideal Viewing Spots

1. Offshore Waters

Whale watching tours venture into offshore waters along the south and west coasts of Oahu, where humpback whales can be spotted breaching, playing, and nurturing their young. Key areas include waters near Diamond Head, Ko Olina, and beyond.

2. Spectacular Encounters

The tours provide opportunities for close encounters, allowing visitors to witness these gentle giants in their natural habitat, often alongside their calves.

Tips for Whale Watching

1. Patience and Timing

Patience is key, as sightings are not guaranteed on every tour. However, whale behavior can be unpredictable, making each sighting a unique experience. Early morning or sunset tours might offer quieter seas and stunning lighting for optimal viewing.

2. Responsible Viewing

Responsible whale watching practices emphasize maintaining a respectful distance from the whales to avoid causing distress or disruption to their natural behaviors. Strict regulations exist to protect these endangered species, and tour operators abide by these guidelines.

Conclusion

Whale watching tours in Honolulu offer a captivating opportunity to witness the grace and beauty of humpback whales during their annual migration. These tours not only provide memorable encounters with these magnificent creatures but also offer educational insights into their behaviors and the importance of marine conservation. For visitors seeking a thrilling and awe-inspiring experience amidst Hawaii's pristine waters, a whale watching tour in Honolulu during the winter months promises an unforgettable glimpse into the world of these gentle giants of the sea.

SUNSET CRUISES IN HONOLULU: SAILING INTO SERENITY

Sunset Splendor

1. Mesmerizing Views

Honolulu's sunset cruises offer unparalleled views of the sun dipping below the horizon, casting vibrant colors across the sky and reflecting on the tranquil waters. The Pacific Ocean serves as a canvas for nature's stunning spectacle.

2. Romantic Atmosphere

Sunset cruises create a romantic ambiance, making them an ideal experience for couples, honeymooners, or those seeking a serene evening with loved ones. The soothing sea breeze and serene setting evoke a sense of tranquility and romance.

Cruise Experiences

1. Catamaran Cruises

Several tour companies offer catamaran cruises departing from Waikiki or nearby harbors, providing comfortable and spacious decks for optimal sunset viewing. Live music, complimentary drinks, and light snacks often enhance the cruising experience.

2. Dinner Cruises

Some sunset cruises include dinner options, allowing guests to savor delectable meals while enjoying the panoramic views. Gourmet dining experiences amidst the ocean's backdrop create an unforgettable evening.

Iconic Locations

1. Waikiki Beach

Cruises departing from Waikiki Beach offer stunning views of Diamond Head and the city skyline as the sun sets behind the iconic volcanic crater. The lively ambiance of Waikiki adds to the allure of these cruises.

2. Offshore Scenic Routes

Cruises often take scenic routes along Oahu's coastline, providing glimpses of secluded bays, cliffs, and landmarks bathed in the golden light of the setting sun. Opportunities for spotting marine life, such as dolphins or sea turtles, might also arise.

Practical Tips

1. Booking and Timing

Sunset cruises are popular, so booking in advance is recommended to secure a spot, especially during peak seasons. Arrive early to ensure ample time to board and settle in for the sunset spectacle.

2. Attire and Comfort

Dress comfortably and in layers to accommodate potential changes in temperature as the evening progresses. Don't forget sunscreen and hats to protect against the fading sunlight.

Unforgettable Memories

1. Photo Opportunities

Sunset cruises offer prime opportunities for capturing stunning photographs of the picturesque sunset against the ocean backdrop.

Don't miss the chance to document the captivating moments.

2. Relaxation and Enjoyment

Embrace the moment and relish the serenity of the ocean as the sun paints the sky with a kaleidoscope of colors. Unplug and unwind, allowing the beauty of the sunset to create lasting memories.

Conclusion

Sunset cruises in Honolulu present an enchanting way to witness nature's grandeur as the sun bids farewell to the day. Whether aboard a catamaran or a dinner cruise, the experience promises unparalleled views and a sense of tranquility that lingers long after the sun has set. For visitors seeking a serene and romantic escape or simply a peaceful evening at sea, a sunset cruise in Honolulu is a journey into the enchanting beauty of the Pacific Ocean's twilight hours.

5

DINING AND CUISINE

EXPLORING HAWAIIAN CUISINE: A FUSION OF FLAVORS

Iconic Dishes

1. Kalua Pig

Slow-roasted in an underground pit known as an imu, Kalua pig is a traditional Hawaiian dish, tender and smoky in flavor. Served during special occasions, luaus, and gatherings, it's a staple of Hawaiian feasts.

2. Poke

Poke (pronounced poh-keh) is a popular dish consisting of marinated raw fish (often tuna) seasoned with soy sauce, sesame oil, onions, and other spices.

Served as an appetizer or a main dish, poke showcases Hawaii's affinity for fresh seafood.

Unique Flavors

1. Locally Sourced Ingredients

Hawaiian cuisine emphasizes fresh, locally sourced ingredients such as taro, coconut, sweet potatoes, and tropical fruits like pineapple, mango, and guava. The use of these ingredients infuses dishes with distinct Hawaiian flavors.

2. Fusion of Cultures

Hawaiian cuisine is a fusion of various cultural influences, including Native Hawaiian, Polynesian, Asian (particularly Japanese and Chinese), Portuguese, and Filipino cuisines.

This fusion results in dishes like loco moco (a dish with rice, hamburger patty, eggs, and gravy) and malasadas (Portuguese-style doughnuts).

Plate Lunch

1. Iconic Meal

Plate lunch, a local favorite, typically consists of a protein (such as chicken, beef, or seafood) served with rice and macaroni salad. Often found at local eateries known as "plate lunch spots," it's a filling and affordable meal.

2. Spam Musubi

A unique Hawaiian snack, spam musubi is made by layering a slice of grilled Spam on a block of rice, wrapped together with nori (seaweed). This snack reflects the influence of Spam introduced during World War II and has become a local favorite.

Culinary Influences

1. Asian Influence

Asian culinary techniques and ingredients, particularly from Japan and China, have heavily influenced Hawaiian cooking, seen in dishes like saimin (noodle soup) and dim sum.

2. Portuguese Heritage

Portuguese immigrants introduced dishes like malasadas (fried dough) and the iconic sweet bread known as pao doce, which have become integral to Hawaiian cuisine.

Culinary Experiences

1. Local Eateries and Food Trucks

Exploring local eateries and food trucks allows visitors to taste authentic Hawaiian cuisine, often prepared by locals using traditional recipes. These establishments offer a wide array of dishes, providing an immersive culinary experience.

2. Farmers' Markets

Visiting farmers' markets offers the chance to sample fresh produce, tropical fruits, and homemade treats, providing a glimpse into the vibrant local food culture.

Conclusion

Hawaiian cuisine is a celebration of diverse flavors, cultural influences, and locally sourced ingredients that reflect the unique heritage of the islands. From traditional dishes like Kalua pig and poke to fusion favorites such as plate lunches and spam musubi, the culinary landscape of Hawaii is a vibrant tapestry of flavors waiting to be savored. Exploring local eateries, food trucks, and farmers' markets is not just about tasting the cuisine but also experiencing the rich cultural heritage and warmth of Hawaii's culinary traditions.

BEST RESTAURANTS AND CAFES

RESTAURANTS

1. Ramen Akatsuki

    2250 Kalākaua Avenue LL 100-1, Honolulu, HI 96815

    +1 808-888-0011

2. Tempura Kiki

    2250 Kalākaua Ave LL#6, Honolulu, HI 96815

    www.tempurakiki.com

    +1 808-888-0514

3. STRIPSTEAK Waikiki

    2330 Kalākaua Ave #330, Honolulu, HI 96815

www.michaelmina.net

+1 808-896-2545

4. Momosan Waikiki

2490 Kalākaua Ave, Honolulu, HI 96815

www.momosanramen.com

+1 808-922-0011

5. Azure

2259 Kalākaua Ave, Honolulu, HI 96815

www.azurewaikiki.com

+1 808-921-4600

6. Hy's Steak House - Waikiki

2440 Kūhiō Ave., Honolulu, HI 96815

www.hyshawaii.com

+1 808-922-5555

7. Ruth's Chris Steak House

226 Lewers St, Waikiki, HI 96815

www.ruthschris.com

+1 808-440-7910

8. South Shore Grill

3114 Monsarrat Ave, Honolulu, HI 96815

www.southshoregrill.com

+1 808-734-0229

9. Orchids

2199 Kālia Rd, Honolulu, HI 96815

www.halekulani.com

+1 808-923-2311

10. Side Street Inn

614 Kapahulu Ave #100, Honolulu, HI 96815

sidestreetinn.com

+1 808-739-3939

CAFES

1. Kona Coffee Purveyors

   Kuhio Avenue Mall Entrance at International Marketplace, 2330 Kalākaua Ave #160, Honolulu, HI 96815

   www.konacoffeepurveyors.com

   +1 808-450-2364

2. Cafe Kaila

2919 Kapiolani Blvd, Honolulu, HI 96816

www.cafe-kaila-hawaii.com

+1 808-732-3330

3. Kai Coffee Hawaii

2490 Kalākaua Ave, Honolulu, HI 96815

www.kaicoffeehawaii.com

+1 808-926-1131

4. Koko Head Cafe

1120 12th Ave #100, Honolulu, HI 96816

www.kokoheadcafe.com

+1 808-732-8920

5. Honolulu Coffee

1800 Kalākaua Ave, Honolulu, HI 96815

www.honolulucoffee.com

+1 808-202-2562

DIETARY OPTIONS AND SPECIALTIES IN HONOLULU

Vegan and Vegetarian Options

Ai Love Nalo: Known for its vegan dishes using locally sourced ingredients, offering items like jackfruit tacos and acai bowls.

Peace Cafe: Offers an all-vegan menu with plant-based versions of Hawaiian dishes like loco moco and a variety of smoothie bowls.

Juicy Brew: A vegan-friendly cafe serving fresh juices, smoothies, and acai bowls, along with vegan pastries.

Gluten-Free Choices

Aloha Salads: Provides a range of customizable salads and wraps with gluten-free options, emphasizing fresh, locally sourced ingredients.

Down to Earth: A natural food store and cafe offering a wide selection of gluten-free products, including prepared foods and baked goods.

Seafood and Poke Specialties

Poke Bar: Offers a variety of poke bowls with fresh seafood selections, allowing customization with different toppings and sauces.

Maguro Brothers: Known for its high-quality and fresh sashimi and poke bowls made from locally caught fish.

Traditional Hawaiian Cuisine

Ono Hawaiian Foods: A classic spot for traditional Hawaiian cuisine, serving dishes like laulau, poi, and kalua pig.

Helena's Hawaiian Food: Provides authentic Hawaiian fare, including squid luau, lomi salmon, and pipikaula (Hawaiian-style beef jerky).

Fusion and International Flavors

The Pig & The Lady: Offers Vietnamese-inspired cuisine with a Hawaiian twist, featuring dishes like pho French dip and inventive fusion dishes.

Nanzan GiroGiro: A Japanese restaurant with a modern twist, offering an ever-changing menu and inventive dishes influenced by local Hawaiian ingredients.

Health-Conscious Options

Arvo: A health-focused cafe with nutritious options, serving acai bowls, toasts, and specialty coffee drinks.

Kokua Market Natural Foods: A natural food store offering organic produce, gluten-free options, and a variety of health-conscious products.

FOOD TRUCKS WITH VARIOUS OPTIONS

Eat Da Bowl: A food truck offering customizable bowls with diverse options, including vegan, vegetarian, and seafood choices.

Da Spot: A food truck known for its diverse menu, catering to various dietary preferences with options like teriyaki tofu and curry plates.

Local Snacks and Desserts

Leonard's Bakery: Famous for its malasadas (Portuguese doughnuts) available in various flavors, including the classic cinnamon sugar.

Matsumoto Shave Ice: A legendary spot for shave ice, offering a multitude of flavors and combinations.

Coffee Shops and Cafes with Varied Offerings

Island Vintage Coffee: Known for its Hawaiian coffee beans and a selection of healthy bites, smoothies, and acai bowls.

Morning Glass Coffee + Cafe: Offers gourmet coffee and breakfast options like loco moco, catering to various dietary preferences.

Special Dietary Needs Catering

Tucker & Bevvy: Provides options for paleo, keto, and gluten-free diets, offering a variety of salads, sandwiches, and healthy bowls.

Vegan Hills: A vegan restaurant with a menu designed to accommodate various dietary needs, including soy-free and gluten-free options.

These establishments in Honolulu showcase a diverse array of culinary offerings, catering to various dietary preferences, from vegan and gluten-free options to traditional Hawaiian specialties and international fusion flavors. Whether exploring local Hawaiian dishes or seeking health-conscious choices, there are plenty of options to savor the diverse and delicious cuisine in Honolulu.

6
ENTERTAINMENT-LIVE MUSIC VENUES IN HONOLULU

Blue Note Hawaii

A premier jazz club featuring renowned local and international jazz artists, as well as performances from other music genres. Offers an intimate setting with great acoustics, along with a dinner menu for a complete evening experience.

2335 Kalākaua Ave, Honolulu, HI 96815
www.bluenotehawaii.com

+1 808-777-4890

The Republik

A versatile venue hosting diverse musical acts, from indie bands to electronic DJs and hip-hop artists.

Known for its energetic atmosphere and capacity for both large and intimate concerts.

1349 Kapiolani Blvd #30th, Honolulu, HI 96814

www.jointherepublik.com

+1 808-941-7469

Mai Tai Bar

Offers live music performances in an open-air setting overlooking the ocean, often featuring local bands and solo artists. A relaxed ambiance with a selection of tropical cocktails and bar bites.

2259 Kalākaua Ave, Honolulu, HI 96815

www.maitaibarwaikiki.com

+1 808-931-8641

Hawaii Theatre Center

A historic theater hosting a range of performances, including live music events featuring local artists and visiting acts. Known for its beautiful architecture and excellent acoustics, providing an immersive experience for concert-goers.

1130 Bethel St, Honolulu, HI 96813
www.hawaiitheatre.com

+1 808-528-0506

Lulu's Waikiki

A lively bar and restaurant offering nightly live music performances, including cover bands, acoustic sets, and DJs. Known for its energetic atmosphere, beachfront location, and variety of musical entertainment.

2586 Kalākaua Ave, Honolulu, HI 96815
www.luluswaikiki.com

+1 808-926-5222

Downbeat Diner & Lounge

A cozy spot hosting live music nights featuring local bands and open mic events, offering a mix of genres from rock to indie and jazz. A laid-back environment with comfort food and vegetarian options on the menu.

42 N Hotel St, Honolulu, HI 96817
downbeatdiner.com

+1 808-533-2328

The Dragon Upstairs

A speakeasy-style jazz club hosting live jazz and blues performances, along with occasional poetry readings and open mic nights. Known for its intimate setting and showcasing local talent.

1038 Nuuanu Ave, Honolulu, HI 96817
+1 808-526-1411

RumFire

A beachfront lounge featuring live music, including acoustic sets and DJs spinning tunes against the backdrop of the ocean. Offers a vibrant nightlife scene with cocktails and a fire pit for a relaxed evening by the beach.

2255 Kalākaua Ave, Honolulu, HI 96815
www.rumfirewaikiki.com

7

DAY TRIPS AND EXCURSIONS

NORTH SHORE ADVENTURE DAY TRIP

Morning:

Departure from Honolulu: Start your day early to make the most of the trip.

Breakfast in Haleiwa: Begin with a delicious breakfast at one of Haleiwa's local cafes or food trucks.

Mid-Morning:

Surfing Lesson or Beach Time: Engage in a surfing lesson at spots like Haleiwa Beach Park or simply relax on the beautiful North Shore beaches.

Explore Haleiwa Town: Wander through the charming town, browsing art galleries, boutiques, and grabbing some famous shaved ice.

Lunchtime:

Local Eateries: Enjoy a casual lunch at one of the local shrimp trucks or plate lunch spots in the area for authentic Hawaiian flavors.

Afternoon:

Visit Waimea Valley: Explore Waimea Valley, walk the botanical gardens, learn about cultural practices, and take a refreshing dip in Waimea Falls.

Kualoa Ranch Tour: Head to Kualoa Ranch for an adventurous ATV tour, horseback riding, or a jungle expedition amidst stunning landscapes and movie sets.

Sunset:

Sunset Beach: Drive along the coast to Sunset Beach, renowned for its stunning sunsets and relaxed atmosphere.

Sunset Picnic: Pack a picnic or grab dinner at one of the local food trucks and enjoy a beachside sunset picnic.

Evening:

Return to Honolulu: Depart from the North Shore, taking in the scenic drive back to Honolulu as the day comes to an end.

This day trip to Oahu's North Shore provides a blend of outdoor activities, cultural experiences, beach relaxation, and picturesque landscapes, offering a taste of the diverse attractions and adventures that the island has to offer. Adjust the itinerary based on personal preferences and the season to make the most out of your North Shore adventure.

OAHU ISLAND HIGHLIGHTS DAY TRIP

Morning:

Departure from Honolulu: Leave early in the morning to maximize your time.

Diamond Head Hike: Start the day with a hike up Diamond Head for panoramic views of Honolulu and the coastline.

Late Morning:

Poke Breakfast: Grab a quick breakfast of fresh poke (marinated raw fish) at a local market or eatery.

Midday:

Pearl Harbor: Visit the Pearl Harbor Historic Sites, including the USS Arizona Memorial and USS Missouri Battleship.

Lunch at a Food Truck: Enjoy lunch from a food truck, sampling local Hawaiian specialties like garlic shrimp or plate lunches.

Afternoon:

Hanauma Bay: Head to Hanauma Bay Nature Preserve for snorkeling or simply enjoy the scenic views if not into snorkeling.

Drive Along the East Coast: Take a scenic drive along the east coast, passing by scenic lookouts and lush landscapes.

Evening:

Sunset at Waikiki Beach: Return to Waikiki Beach in time for sunset, enjoy a stroll along the beach, and witness the vibrant colors of the sunset.

Dinner in Waikiki: Indulge in a dinner at a beachfront restaurant in Waikiki, savoring the evening ambiance.

Nighttime:

City Lights Drive: Take a drive around downtown Honolulu to see the city lights and nightlife before heading back.

This condensed day trip covers the island's major highlights, from historic sites and natural wonders to stunning viewpoints and cultural experiences. While a single day isn't enough to fully explore everything, this itinerary provides a glimpse into the diverse attractions that Oahu has to offer. Adjustments can be made based on personal interests and preferences for a more tailored experience.

POLYNESIAN CULTURAL CENTER DAY TRIP

Morning:

Departure from Honolulu: Begin early to make the most of your day.

Scenic Drive to Laie: Enjoy the scenic drive to Laie, where the Polynesian Cultural Center is located.

Late Morning:

Arrival at the Cultural Center: Upon arrival, explore the different villages representing various Polynesian cultures, including Samoa, Fiji, Tahiti, and more.

Cultural Presentations: Attend cultural presentations, interactive exhibits, and traditional demonstrations to learn about Polynesian customs, dance, music, and crafts.

Midday:

Lunch: Enjoy a buffet lunch featuring Polynesian and local Hawaiian dishes within the Cultural Center's premises.

Afternoon:

Canoe Pageant: Witness the colorful canoe pageant featuring traditional dances and music from different Polynesian islands.

Activities and Workshops: Engage in hands-on activities, such as lei making, coconut husking, or ukulele lessons, to further immerse yourself in the culture.

Evening:

Polynesian Cultural Show: Watch the famous evening show, "Ha: Breath of Life," a spectacular performance showcasing Polynesian music, dance, and storytelling.

Dinner: Conclude your visit with an optional dinner at the Cultural Center or head back to Honolulu for dinner.

Nighttime:

Return to Honolulu: Depart from the Polynesian Cultural Center, enjoying the scenic drive back to Honolulu in the evening.

A day trip to Ko Olina Resort Area presents a mix of relaxation, beach activities, and luxurious amenities. Here's a suggested itinerary for a day excursion to this beautiful resort area:

KO OLINA RESORT AREA DAY TRIP

Morning:

Departure from Honolulu: Start your day early to maximize your time.

Drive to Ko Olina: Enjoy a scenic drive to Ko Olina, located on the western coast of Oahu.

Late Morning:

Arrival at Ko Olina: Upon arrival, head to one of the four stunning lagoons in Ko Olina for a morning of beach relaxation and water activities.

Beach Time: Relax on the white sand beaches, swim in the crystal-clear waters, or engage in water sports like snorkeling or paddleboarding.

Midday:

Lunch at a Resort Restaurant: Indulge in a leisurely lunch at one of the resort's restaurants or beachside cafes, enjoying ocean views and fresh seafood.

Afternoon:

Lagoon Activities: Explore the different lagoons and their unique features. Some offer calm waters ideal for swimming, while others might have opportunities for more adventurous activities.

Golf or Spa: If interested, consider playing a round of golf at Ko Olina Golf Club or pamper yourself with a spa treatment at one of the resort's spas.

Evening:

Sunset Sail or Dinner Cruise: Consider booking a sunset sail or dinner cruise departing from Ko Olina, offering picturesque views of the sunset over the ocean.

Fine Dining Experience: Enjoy a gourmet dinner at one of the upscale restaurants within the resort area.

Nighttime:

Return to Honolulu: Depart from Ko Olina in the evening, soaking in the last views of the coastline during the drive back to Honolulu.

This day trip to Ko Olina Resort Area offers a luxurious escape with pristine beaches, water activities, fine dining, and opportunities for relaxation amidst the stunning coastal scenery. Tailor the itinerary to your preferences and interests to make the most out of your visit to this beautiful resort destination.

8

FAMILY-FRIENDLY ACTIVITIES

KID-FRIENDLY ATTRACTIONS ON OAHU

Waikiki Beach

Beach Activities: Waikiki's calm waters are perfect for children to swim and play.

Sandcastle Building: Building sandcastles on the beach is a popular and fun activity for kids.

Honolulu Zoo

Animal Encounters: Explore the zoo's diverse collection of animals, including lions, giraffes, elephants, and more.

Keiki (Kids) Zoo: Specifically designed for kids, offering interactive exhibits and activities.

Waikiki Aquarium

Marine Exploration: Discover marine life through interactive exhibits and hands-on experiences.

Daily Programs: Enjoy daily educational programs and feeding sessions for kids to learn about sea creatures.

Kualoa Ranch

Jungle Expedition: Take a jungle expedition tour where kids can see movie set locations, ride ATVs, or embark on a nature hike.

Horseback Riding: Horseback riding tours offer a gentle adventure through beautiful landscapes.

Dole Plantation

Pineapple Express Train Ride: Enjoy a train ride through pineapple fields while learning about the plantation's history.

Maze and Gardens: Get lost in the world's largest maze and explore beautiful gardens.

Sea Life Park

Dolphin Encounters: Watch dolphin shows and even have the chance to interact with these friendly creatures.

Aquarium Exhibits: Explore various aquarium exhibits showcasing marine life.

Bishop Museum

Hawaiian Culture: Engage kids in learning about Hawaiian history, culture, and traditions.

Interactive Exhibits: Hands-on exhibits and programs make learning fun.

Children's Discovery Center

Interactive Museum: Features interactive exhibits, play areas, and educational programs for kids.

Hands-on Learning: Kids can engage in different activities, including arts, crafts, and science experiments.

Aulani, A Disney Resort & Spa

Character Experiences: Meet Disney characters and enjoy themed activities and entertainment.

Pools and Water Play: The resort offers pools, waterslides, and splash zones designed for kids.

Beaches with Tide Pools

Tide Pool Exploration: Visit beaches like Shark's Cove or Kuilima Cove to explore tide pools with kids.

Observing Marine Life: Children can safely observe and learn about small marine creatures.

Botanical Gardens

Exploration and Picnics: Foster Botanical Garden or Hoʻomaluhia Botanical Garden offer beautiful landscapes for exploration and picnics.

Nature Trails: Walk along nature trails and introduce kids to diverse plant life.

These attractions offer a blend of educational experiences, outdoor adventures, and entertainment tailored for children, ensuring a memorable and enjoyable time for the whole family on the island of Oahu.

FAMILY-ORIENTED TOURS ON OAHU

Atlantis Submarine Tour

Submarine Adventure: Take a submarine tour for an underwater exploration, allowing kids to see marine life up close.

Educational Experience: Learn about underwater ecosystems and see sunken shipwrecks.

Catamaran Cruise

Snorkeling Excursion: Join a catamaran cruise offering snorkeling opportunities for the whole family.

Dolphin Watching: Some tours include the chance to spot dolphins in their natural habitat.

Waimea Valley Adventure

Nature Exploration: Visit Waimea Valley for a guided nature tour suitable for families, exploring botanical gardens, waterfalls, and cultural sites.

Swimming Opportunity: Swim in natural pools under the waterfall.

Manoa Chocolate Factory Tour

Chocolate Making: Join a tour of the chocolate factory where kids can learn how chocolate is made from bean to bar.

Interactive Experience: Engage in hands-on activities and tastings.

Helicopter Tour

Aerial Views: Take a helicopter tour to witness breathtaking aerial views of Oahu, including waterfalls, coastlines, and volcanic landscapes.

Educational Commentary: Some tours offer educational commentary suitable for kids.

Surf Lessons

Surfing Experience: Enroll in family-friendly surf lessons at Waikiki Beach or the North Shore.

Instructors for Kids: Experienced instructors tailor lessons for different ages, making it fun and safe.

Shangri La Tour

Cultural Experience: Explore Shangri La, the former estate of Doris Duke, featuring Islamic art and architecture.

Guided Tours: Engaging tours are available, highlighting the cultural and artistic significance.

Bike Tours

Scenic Rides: Enjoy family-friendly bike tours, like riding along the Kamehameha Highway on the North Shore or through the streets of Honolulu.

Bike Rentals: Rent bikes to explore at your own pace or join guided tours.

Hawaiian Fire Luau

Traditional Luau: Experience a family-oriented luau with fire dancers, traditional Polynesian performances, and a feast.

Kid-Friendly Activities: Some luaus offer activities like lei-making and hula lessons for kids.

Pearl Harbor Tours

Historical Exploration: Visit Pearl Harbor with tours catered for families, including the USS Arizona Memorial and interactive exhibits.

Educational Guides: Guides provide insights into history suitable for kids.

Farm Tours

Educational Experience: Explore farms like Kahuku Farms or Aloun Farms with guided tours showcasing local agriculture and offering tastings.

Hands-on Learning: Kids can learn about farming, try fresh fruits, and feed animals.

These family-oriented tours on Oahu cater to different interests, providing educational experiences, outdoor adventures, cultural explorations, and plenty of fun activities suitable for families with kids of all ages.

Beaches and Parks for Families on Oahu

Waikiki Beach

Family-Friendly Atmosphere: Shallow waters and gentle waves make it perfect for kids.

Activities: Offers opportunities for swimming, sandcastle building, and beach games.

Kapiolani Park

Playgrounds: Features playgrounds and open spaces for picnics and games.

Honolulu Zoo: Located nearby, allowing families to combine beach and zoo outings.

Ala Moana Beach Park

Sheltered Lagoon: Has a sheltered area ideal for families with young children.

Picnic Areas: Offers picnic spots, shady trees, and grassy areas for relaxation.

Lanikai Beach

Calmer Waters: Clear waters and gentle currents make it suitable for families.

Pillbox Hike: Older kids can enjoy a hike for panoramic views (consider kids' endurance for this trail).

Ko Olina Lagoons

Man-Made Lagoons: Offers calm waters perfect for swimming and snorkeling with kids.

Resort Amenities: Access to nearby resorts with restaurants and facilities.

Hanauma Bay Nature Preserve

Snorkeling: Older kids can enjoy snorkeling and seeing colorful fish in the protected bay.

Educational Center: Teaches about marine life and conservation.

Waimea Bay Beach Park

Rock Jumping: Older kids can enjoy rock jumping when the waves are calm.

Picnic Areas: Offers picnic spots with shaded areas.

Makapuu Beach Park

Tide Pools: Explore tide pools with kids and discover marine life.

Lighthouse Trail: Older kids might enjoy a hike to the lighthouse for scenic views.

Magic Island

Lagoon Area: Offers a calm lagoon suitable for kids to wade and swim.

Green Space: Wide green spaces perfect for picnics and outdoor games.

Waimanalo Bay Beach Park

Sandy Beach: Soft sands and clear waters make it suitable for families.

Pristine Setting: Offers a more secluded and less crowded atmosphere.

Diamond Head Beach Park

Tide Pools: Great for exploring tide pools and observing sea creatures.

Beachcombing: Kids can collect shells and beach treasures.

These beaches and parks on Oahu offer a mix of amenities, gentle waters, beautiful landscapes, and family-friendly environments, ensuring a fantastic day out for families looking to enjoy the island's natural beauty and outdoor activities.

9

PRACTICAL INFORMATION

SAFETY TIPS FOR FAMILIES VISITING OAHU

Beach Safety

Swimming Vigilance: Always supervise children while swimming and stay within designated swimming areas.

Water Conditions: Be aware of changing tide conditions and strong currents, especially on the North Shore.

Sun Protection: Use sunscreen, hats, and UV-protective clothing to prevent sunburn.

Water Activities

Snorkeling Safety: Provide children with proper-fitting snorkel gear and stay together in shallow, calm waters.

Life Jackets: Ensure young children wear appropriate life jackets or floatation devices for water activities.

Hiking and Exploring

Stay on Trails: Stick to marked trails while hiking to avoid getting lost or encountering hazards.

Prepare Essentials: Bring water, snacks, appropriate footwear, and sun protection for hikes.

Know Limits: Choose hikes suitable for your family's fitness level and kids' endurance.

General Safety

Stay Hydrated: Keep hydrated, especially in warm weather, by drinking plenty of water.

Emergency Contacts: Keep emergency contact information handy and be aware of nearest medical facilities.

Buddy System: Use the buddy system and set meeting points in case family members get separated.

Traffic and Transportation

Road Safety: Use crosswalks and pedestrian pathways, and always hold hands with children when crossing streets.

Car Seat Safety: Ensure proper use of car seats and seat belts for children in vehicles.

Cultural Awareness

Respect Local Customs: Familiarize kids with local customs and cultural practices to promote respect and understanding.

Language Barriers: Consider language differences and have a few basic phrases in Hawaiian if possible.

Wildlife Caution

Respect Marine Life: Admire marine life from a safe distance while snorkeling or exploring tide pools.

Watch for Hazards: Be cautious of potentially hazardous creatures, like jellyfish, while in the water.

COVID-19 Precautions

Follow Guidelines: Adhere to local health guidelines regarding masks, social distancing, and hygiene practices.

Check Restrictions: Be aware of any travel restrictions or specific COVID-19 guidelines in place during your visit.

Local Guidance

Ask Locals: Seek advice from locals or tour guides for safety tips and advice on specific locations or activities.

LOCAL CUSTOMS AND ETIQUETTE IN HAWAII

Respect for 'Aloha Spirit'

Aloha Greeting: 'Aloha' means more than just hello; it embodies warmth, kindness, and love. Use it genuinely.

Respect and Politeness: Show respect and kindness to everyone you encounter.

Removing Shoes Indoors

Shoes Off: It's customary to remove shoes before entering someone's home in Hawaii.

Respect for Cleanliness: Helps keep homes clean and respects the Hawaiian value of 'noho 'olu' (sitting comfortably).

Sharing and Generosity

Sharing Culture: Hawaiians value sharing food, stories, and experiences.

Mahalo (Thank You): Express gratitude often; saying 'mahalo' is customary and appreciated.

Clothing and Attire

Casual Dress: Hawaii's atmosphere is generally casual; beachwear is acceptable in appropriate settings.

Respectful Dress: When visiting sacred sites or attending formal events, opt for modest attire.

Litter-Free Environment

Malama 'Aina (Respecting the Land): Maintain a clean environment; dispose of trash properly.

Leave No Trace: Practice 'kokua' (helping hand) by leaving places as you found them.

Cultural Sites and Sacred Places

Respectful Behavior: Show reverence at sacred sites; follow posted guidelines and signs.

No Littering or Touching: Avoid touching or disturbing artifacts or natural formations.

LEARNING HAWAIIAN PHRASES

Basic Greetings: Learning a few Hawaiian phrases like 'aloha' (hello/goodbye) or 'mahalo' (thank you) is appreciated.

Respectful Acknowledgment: Pronouncing local names and places respectfully shows cultural awareness.

Punctuality and Relaxed Pace

'Hawaiian Time': Embrace the relaxed pace; punctuality is valued, but events may start a bit later than scheduled.

Patience and Flexibility: Embrace a more laid-back approach to schedules and plans.

Parking and Driving Etiquette

Sharing Parking: Be courteous when parking; spaces can be limited in certain areas.

Aloha on the Road: Use the 'shaka' (hang loose) gesture to thank drivers; it's a friendly and common gesture.

Photography Etiquette

Respectful Photography: Seek permission before taking photos of locals or cultural ceremonies.

Ask Before Sharing: Respect people's privacy; ask before posting images of individuals.

EMERGENCY CONTACTS FOR OAHU

Police, Fire, Medical Emergencies

Emergency Services: Dial 911 for immediate assistance in case of any emergency (Police, Fire, Medical).

Hospitals and Medical Centers

The Queen's Medical Center:

Address: 1301 Punchbowl St, Honolulu, HI 96813

Phone: +1 808-691-1000

Straub Medical Center:

Address: 888 S King St, Honolulu, HI 96813

Phone: +1 808-522-4000

Non-Emergency Services

Honolulu Police Department Non-Emergency:

Phone: +1 808-529-3111

Fire Department Non-Emergency:

Phone: +1 808-723-7139

U.S. Coast Guard

Coast Guard Search and Rescue:

Phone: +1 808-842-2600

Poison Control

Hawaii Poison Hotline:

Phone: +1 800-222-1222

Embassy Contacts

Consulate General of Japan:

Phone: +1 808-543-3111

Consulate General of the Republic of Korea:

Phone: +1 808-595-6109

Consulate General of the Philippines:

Phone: +1 808-595-6316

Travel Assistance

Traveler's Insurance or Tour Operator: Contact your travel insurance provider or tour operator for assistance during emergencies or medical needs.

Taxis or Ride-Sharing Services

Local Taxi Services or Ride-Sharing Apps: Always keep local transportation services handy for urgent travel needs.

Local Accommodation

Hotel or Accommodation Reception: Front desks often have emergency protocols and can assist in case of any urgent situations.

It's wise to keep these emergency contacts stored in your phone or written down in case of unforeseen circumstances during your visit to Oahu. Additionally, ensure that someone trusted within your group knows where to find these contacts in case of an emergency.

Sure, learning a few phrases in Hawaiian can enhance your experience and show respect for the local culture. Here are some useful phrases:

USEFUL PHRASES IN HAWAIIAN

Greetings and Basics

Aloha (ah-LOH-hah) - Hello, goodbye, love, affection.

Mahalo (mah-HAH-loh) - Thank you.

'A'ole pilikia (AH-oh-leh pee-lee-KEE-ah) - You're welcome, no problem.

Pehea 'oe? (peh-HAY-ah OH-eh) - How are you?

Maika'i no au (my-KAH-ee noh ow) - I'm fine/good.

Polite Expressions

'O wai kou inoa? (oh VAI koh EE-noh-ah) - What is your name?

'O [Your Name] ko'u inoa (oh [Your Name] KOH-oo EE-noh-ah) - My name is [Your Name].

E kala mai (eh KAH-lah MY) - Excuse me, sorry.

'O 'oe ka mea nui (oh OH-eh kah MEH-ah NOO-ee) - You are important.

Directions and Essentials

Kahi malu (KA-hee MAH-loo) - Restroom.

Aia ma hea...? (AI-ah mah HAY-ah) - Where is...?

Makai (mah-KAI) - Toward the ocean.

Mauka (MOW-kah) - Toward the mountains.

Food and Drinks

Ono (OH-noh) - Delicious.

Pūpū (POO-poo) - Appetizer, snack.

Nui (NOO-ee) - Large, big.

I'a (EE-ah) - Fish.

Numbers

'Ekahi (eh-KAH-hee) - One.

'Elua (eh-LOO-ah) - Two.

'Ekolu (eh-KOH-loo) - Three.

'Eha (EH-hah) - Four.

'Elima (eh-LEE-mah) - Five.

Expressions of Affection

Aloha nui loa (ah-LOH-hah NOO-ee LOH-ah) - Much love, deepest affection.

Aloha au ia 'oe (ah-LOH-hah ow EE-ah OH-eh) - I love you.

Parting Expressions

A hui hou (ah HOO-ee HOH-oo) - Until we meet again.

Aloha 'oe (ah-LOH-hah OH-eh) - Farewell to you.

BONUS

HONOLULU TRAVEL PLANNER

Date:
Location:
Budget:

ITINERARY

TODAY'S LOG

6 AM
7 AM
8 AM
9 AM
10 AM
11 AM
12 PM
1 PM
2 PM
3 PM
4 PM
5 PM
6 PM
7 PM
8 PM
9 PM
10 PM
11 PM

PLACES TO GO

LOCAL FOODS TO TRY

HONOLULU TRAVEL PLANNER

Date:
Location:
Budget:

PLACES TO GO
-
-
-
-

LOCAL FOODS TO TRY
-
-
-
-

ITINERARY
TODAY'S LOG

6 AM	
7 AM	
8 AM	
9 AM	
10 AM	
11 AM	
12 PM	
1 PM	
2 PM	
3 PM	
4 PM	
5 PM	
6 PM	
7 PM	
8 PM	
9 PM	
10 PM	
11 PM	

HONOLULU TRAVEL PLANNER

Date:
Location:
Budget:

PLACES TO GO

LOCAL FOODS TO TRY

ITINERARY

TODAY'S LOG

- 6 AM
- 7 AM
- 8 AM
- 9 AM
- 10 AM
- 11 AM
- 12 PM
- 1 PM
- 2 PM
- 3 PM
- 4 PM
- 5 PM
- 6 PM
- 7 PM
- 8 PM
- 9 PM
- 10 PM
- 11 PM

HONOLULU TRAVEL PLANNER

Date:
Location:
Budget:

ITINERARY

TODAY'S LOG

6 AM
7 AM
8 AM
9 AM
10 AM
11 AM
12 PM
1 PM
2 PM
3 PM
4 PM
5 PM
6 PM
7 PM
8 PM
9 PM
10 PM
11 PM

PLACES TO GO

☐
☐
☐
☐

LOCAL FOODS TO TRY

☐
☐
☐
☐

HONOLULU TRAVEL PLANNER

Date:
Location:
Budget:

PLACES TO GO

LOCAL FOODS TO TRY

ITINERARY

TODAY'S LOG

6 AM
7 AM
8 AM
9 AM
10 AM
11 AM
12 PM
1 PM
2 PM
3 PM
4 PM
5 PM
6 PM
7 PM
8 PM
9 PM
10 PM
11 PM

HONOLULU TRAVEL PLANNER

Date:
Location:
Budget:

PLACES TO GO

LOCAL FOODS TO TRY

ITINERARY

TODAY'S LOG

6 AM
7 AM
8 AM
9 AM
10 AM
11 AM
12 PM
1 PM
2 PM
3 PM
4 PM
5 PM
6 PM
7 PM
8 PM
9 PM
10 PM
11 PM

HONOLULU TRAVEL PLANNER

Date:
Location:
Budget:

ITINERARY

TODAY'S LOG

6 AM
7 AM
8 AM
9 AM
10 AM
11 AM
12 PM
1 PM
2 PM
3 PM
4 PM
5 PM
6 PM
7 PM
8 PM
9 PM
10 PM
11 PM

PLACES TO GO

-
-
-
-

LOCAL FOODS TO TRY

-
-
-
-

HONOLULU TRAVEL PLANNER

Date:
Location:
Budget:

PLACES TO GO

LOCAL FOODS TO TRY

ITINERARY

TODAY'S LOG

| 6 AM |
| 7 AM |
| 8 AM |
| 9 AM |
| 10 AM |
| 11 AM |
| 12 PM |
| 1 PM |
| 2 PM |
| 3 PM |
| 4 PM |
| 5 PM |
| 6 PM |
| 7 PM |
| 8 PM |
| 9 PM |
| 10 PM |
| 11 PM |

HONOLULU TRAVEL PLANNER

Date:
Location:
Budget:

PLACES TO GO
-
-
-
-

LOCAL FOODS TO TRY
-
-
-
-

ITINERARY

TODAY'S LOG

6 AM	
7 AM	
8 AM	
9 AM	
10 AM	
11 AM	
12 PM	
1 PM	
2 PM	
3 PM	
4 PM	
5 PM	
6 PM	
7 PM	
8 PM	
9 PM	
10 PM	
11 PM	

HONOLULU TRAVEL PLANNER

Date:
Location:
Budget:

PLACES TO GO

-
-
-
-

LOCAL FOODS TO TRY

-
-
-
-

ITINERARY

TODAY'S LOG

6 AM	
7 AM	
8 AM	
9 AM	
10 AM	
11 AM	
12 PM	
1 PM	
2 PM	
3 PM	
4 PM	
5 PM	
6 PM	
7 PM	
8 PM	
9 PM	
10 PM	
11 PM	

HONOLULU TRAVEL PLANNER

Date:
Location:
Budget:

ITINERARY

TODAY'S LOG

6 AM
7 AM
8 AM
9 AM
10 AM
11 AM
12 PM
1 PM
2 PM
3 PM
4 PM
5 PM
6 PM
7 PM
8 PM
9 PM
10 PM
11 PM

PLACES TO GO

-
-
-
-

LOCAL FOODS TO TRY

-
-
-
-

HONOLULU TRAVEL PLANNER

Date:
Location:
Budget:

PLACES TO GO

LOCAL FOODS TO TRY

ITINERARY

TODAY'S LOG

- 6 AM
- 7 AM
- 8 AM
- 9 AM
- 10 AM
- 11 AM
- 12 PM
- 1 PM
- 2 PM
- 3 PM
- 4 PM
- 5 PM
- 6 PM
- 7 PM
- 8 PM
- 9 PM
- 10 PM
- 11 PM

HONOLULU TRAVEL PLANNER

Date:
Location:
Budget:

PLACES TO GO
-
-
-
-

LOCAL FOODS TO TRY
-
-
-
-

ITINERARY

TODAY'S LOG

6 AM	
7 AM	
8 AM	
9 AM	
10 AM	
11 AM	
12 PM	
1 PM	
2 PM	
3 PM	
4 PM	
5 PM	
6 PM	
7 PM	
8 PM	
9 PM	
10 PM	
11 PM	

HONOLULU TRAVEL PLANNER

Date:
Location:
Budget:

ITINERARY

TODAY'S LOG

6 AM
7 AM
8 AM
9 AM
10 AM
11 AM
12 PM
1 PM
2 PM
3 PM
4 PM
5 PM
6 PM
7 PM
8 PM
9 PM
10 PM
11 PM

PLACES TO GO

LOCAL FOODS TO TRY

HONOLULU TRAVEL PLANNER

Date:
Location:
Budget:

ITINERARY

TODAY'S LOG

6 AM
7 AM
8 AM
9 AM
10 AM
11 AM
12 PM
1 PM
2 PM
3 PM
4 PM
5 PM
6 PM
7 PM
8 PM
9 PM
10 PM
11 PM

PLACES TO GO

LOCAL FOODS TO TRY

HONOLULU TRAVEL PLANNER

Date:
Location:
Budget:

PLACES TO GO
-
-
-
-

LOCAL FOODS TO TRY
-
-
-
-

ITINERARY

TODAY'S LOG

6 AM	
7 AM	
8 AM	
9 AM	
10 AM	
11 AM	
12 PM	
1 PM	
2 PM	
3 PM	
4 PM	
5 PM	
6 PM	
7 PM	
8 PM	
9 PM	
10 PM	
11 PM	

HONOLULU TRAVEL PLANNER

Date:
Location:
Budget:

PLACES TO GO

LOCAL FOODS TO TRY

ITINERARY

TODAY'S LOG

6 AM
7 AM
8 AM
9 AM
10 AM
11 AM
12 PM
1 PM
2 PM
3 PM
4 PM
5 PM
6 PM
7 PM
8 PM
9 PM
10 PM
11 PM

HONOLULU TRAVEL PLANNER

Date:

Location:

Budget:

PLACES TO GO

LOCAL FOODS TO TRY

ITINERARY

TODAY'S LOG

6 AM
7 AM
8 AM
9 AM
10 AM
11 AM
12 PM
1 PM
2 PM
3 PM
4 PM
5 PM
6 PM
7 PM
8 PM
9 PM
10 PM
11 PM

HONOLULU TRAVEL PLANNER

Date:
Location:
Budget:

PLACES TO GO
-
-
-
-

LOCAL FOODS TO TRY
-
-
-
-

ITINERARY

TODAY'S LOG

6 AM	
7 AM	
8 AM	
9 AM	
10 AM	
11 AM	
12 PM	
1 PM	
2 PM	
3 PM	
4 PM	
5 PM	
6 PM	
7 PM	
8 PM	
9 PM	
10 PM	
11 PM	

HONOLULU TRAVEL PLANNER

Date:
Location:
Budget:

PLACES TO GO

LOCAL FOODS TO TRY

ITINERARY

TODAY'S LOG

6 AM
7 AM
8 AM
9 AM
10 AM
11 AM
12 PM
1 PM
2 PM
3 PM
4 PM
5 PM
6 PM
7 PM
8 PM
9 PM
10 PM
11 PM